Fishing for
MONSTERS

**LUCKY LUKE'S
ADVENTURES**

ENJOY
the
Adventure!!

K—

Illustrated by Darcy Bell-Myers

Softcover ISBN 979-8-9888393-1-6
Hardcover ISBN 979-8-9888393-2-3

Printed in the United States of America

Cover and interior design by James Monroe Design, LLC.

Lucky Luke, LLC.
4335 Matthew Court
Eagan, Minnesota 55123

www.KevinLovegreen.com

Chapter 1

I'm looking out a tiny window of a tiny airplane. The view below me is anything but tiny, though.

We're flying deep into northern Canada. As far as my eyes can see, there are shimmering blue lakes, endless rows of dark-green pine trees, and miles of grassy meadows. It looks like a puzzle, with different-colored pieces randomly scattered and locked together.

As the view stretches below me, I think about the monsters lurking down there in every lake. I don't mean mythical water-beasts like the Loch Ness monster. I mean monster fish. These lakes are home to some of the biggest northern pike you can catch anywhere in the world.

In fact, that's why we're here. Dad and Uncle Vern are on a quest to catch northerns of a lifetime to celebrate Uncle Vern turning forty this year. He and Dad are hoping to land something twenty pounds or even bigger. That's *huge*!

And who knows . . . maybe northerns aren't the only monsters swimming under all that shiny blue water. These lakes are huge, wild, and practically untouched. They could be full of surprises and mysteries. I have a great feeling about this. Maybe, just maybe, we'll be lucky enough to catch an unexpected monster.

After all, they don't call me Lucky Luke for nothing!

Dad taps me on the shoulder. "There it is!" he almost shouts so I can hear him over the roar of the plane. He points out the window.

Below, I see three brown log cabins with red roofs. The cabins are tucked into the edge of a slate-blue lake. I jam my face up to the window to get a better look at the lake itself, but it's hard to see.

Then the pilot—who's a lot younger than I think a pilot should be—turns the plane. Now I have a full view of this magical lake. I see its fingers, islands, and big round bays.

Of the endless lakes I've seen during this hour-long flight, this is one of the largest.

I give Dad a thumbs-up. I know he's as excited as I am. Maybe even more excited.

I then look over at my cousin Dillon, who's sitting across the aisle from me and looking out his own window. I tap him on the knee.

Dill pulls his face away from the window and looks over at me. His giant smile and wild eyes say it all. He nods slowly up and down and gives me a look. I've seen that look many times.

It means, *This is gonna be fun.*

Dillon and I are the same age. He's a little shorter than me, though we couldn't look any different. He has brown hair, and

I have red. He gets tan in the summer, and my mom makes sure I pile on the sunscreen.

But we do have one thing in common: we love to hunt, fish, and do anything outside. We are so lucky that we get to go along on this amazing fishing trip with our dads.

Uncle Vern and Dad do all kinds of hunting and fishing together. Uncle Vern is a little older than Dad. And even though they're brothers, they look as different as Dillon and I do. Dad has red hair, like me. Uncle Vern has brown hair. For the trip, he grew a scruffy bit of a beard. He said he wanted to look "rugged" for the deep woods of Canada.

That isn't the only part of his rugged look. With his brown hat, green sunglasses, and dark-green fishing jacket, he looks like he could be on the cover of a fishing magazine.

Dad also looks the part. He's wearing his Indiana Jones hat, sunglasses, and a brown jacket that's ready for rain, wind, or whatever Mother Nature throws at him.

Both Uncle Vern and Dad love their hunting and fishing gear. Dill and I joke that there's a little brotherly competition between them. They each want to have the best stuff!

Suddenly, the plane drops quickly and banks hard to the left. My stomach jumps. I have to use my left arm to keep my face from smashing against the window.

Then we straighten out and slice through the sky. The green pines below are now in perfect view. It seems like we're dropping right on top of them.

I look out the front window and see a small red clay runway in a landing area about the size of two football fields. The runway doesn't seem much bigger than a driveway. Is it even big enough to land this puddle jumper? I grip my seat and prepare to hit the ground.

The tires touch down. After two quick hops, the tires seem to grab the ground. But we're still moving fast. The trees at the end of the field get bigger and bigger. We're heading right for them!

Then the pilot slams on the brakes. We all launch forward. Thank goodness for my seat belt, or my nose might have hit the pilot in the back of his head.

The pilot looks into the mirror to check on us. He gives us a crazy smile. "Is everyone alive back there?" he shouts over the buzzing propellers.

"Yep!" Dad shouts back. He gives a thumbs-up in case the pilot didn't hear him.

"Well, then, I have done my job," the pilot yells out. "Sorry for the quick stop, though. Runways are a little short out here in the bush. And the trees aren't very friendly if we hit them."

The pilot says this part without a smile. I think he's trying to be funny, but I can't tell for sure.

I look over at Dillon. That crazy-fun look is now replaced with a white face and worried eyes.

Dad, too, sees the look on Dillon's face. "You OK, Dill?"

"Ya, I'm good," Dillon says.

I don't think we believe him.

The plane spins around, and we bounce back down the runway. Eventually, we stop, and the pilot cuts the engine. After an hour of deafening roars, silence finally fills the cab.

"Whew! That is a good sound," Uncle Vern says.

The pilot opens the door, and we all pile out. The crisp Canadian air is filled with the smell of pine. It hits me square in the nose. I smile.

This fishing adventure is just getting revved up!

Chapter 2

Two guys come walking down a dirt trail, each pulling a big black cart. They both wear green jackets that look brand new and feature the lodge's name. And both guys have dark sunglasses, black mustaches, and skin that looks like tanned leather. They're both wearing hats, too, though one hat is camo and the other is light tan.

"Welcome to Webber's Lodge," the first man says. "I'm Jack, and this is Leo."

After some quick introductions, we load our gear onto the carts. We then follow the men back up the path, toward the lodge.

Behind us, the airplane comes back to life. Before long, it shoots out over the lake and into the dark-blue sky. It looks like a giant bird migrating south.

At last, we reach the lodge. It's awesome—it's made from giant pine trees. The logs are huge.

Once we head inside, I'm even more amazed. Everything is made of honey-colored wood. The walls are filled with hunting and fishing trophies. There are giant northerns, huge whitetail bucks, massive caribou, and some grouse and ducks. This place is paradise.

A nice lady with a big smile and long strawberry blond hair welcomes us. "Hi, I'm Jean. My husband, Mike, and I own the lodge. Actually, it's been in my family for over thirty years. I could tell you a lot of stories about this place . . ." She pauses as she smiles over at Dill and me. "But I bet you guys are itching to get unpacked. I'll have lunch ready soon, and then you can head out on the lake!"

Dill and I fly into action. We zip about, unpacking our gear and setting up our fishing rods. Dill and I are so speedy that we even have time to set up our dads' rods too.

Just as we finish, a mouthwatering smell fills the air. It's time for lunch. The big wood table is loaded with food—burgers, baked beans, plump red strawberries, and chocolate pudding.

"I hope you guys like venison burgers," Jean says to Dill and me.

"We love venison!" I say as I sit at the table. I can't hide the big smile on my face.

"All the meat we serve here is something we've hunted or fished ourselves," Jean says.

"Just like at home," Dad says, sliding into a chair. "Wouldn't you say, guys?"

Dill and I both grin and nod. We get busy loading up our plates. I can't wait for that first bite—it melts in my mouth. I don't even care when some ketchup drips down my chin.

Dill and I burn through our food. Our dads, though, take their time and savor every morsel. We wait as patiently as we can, but it's tough. The sooner we finish lunch, the sooner we'll be on the water.

14

Suddenly, we hear a long creaking sound. We look over at the front door.

Jack appears, like a turtle poking his head out of his shell. "The boats are ready whenever you guys are," he says. Then he disappears, like he's pulling his head back into his shell.

Jean comes out of the kitchen, smiling and humming. I'm getting the feeling that she's always happy.

"The fish have been biting lately," she says. "You'd better get out there and go after them!" Her smile widens as she points with her thumb in the direction of the door.

Dill and I jump up and take off running for our gear.

"Stop right there, boys!" Dad calls out.

We slam on the brakes.

"We will be carrying our plates into the kitchen to show this wonderful lady that we have manners," Dad says. "Isn't that right?"

We instantly turn and head back to the table. "Whoops. Sorry," I say. "Where would you like our plates, ma'am?"

"The sink is through that door and to the right," Jean says. "Thank you for being such gentlemen. I'll take it from there." She gives us a wink.

Once our dishes are cleared, Dill and I waste no time racing to our rooms to get our jackets.

Monster northerns, here we come!

Chapter 3

We all march down to the dock, where the red-and-silver sixteen-foot aluminum boats are waiting. Dad and I hop in one boat with Jack, and Uncle Vern and Dill get in the other with Leo.

I pull on a green life jacket and zip it up. Dad does the same.

"Let's do this!" Dad says, giving Jack a thumbs-up.

The motor revs to life with one quick pull from Jack's strong right hand. I push us away from the dock, and then we're off. The boat cuts through the water, making waves the color of apple cider.

I take in the sights as we race down the shoreline. It's a mix of big rocks, giant boulders, and a million green pine trees. Looking in front of us, I can see only water and more water. There's no shoreline on the horizon.

This is a *big* lake. And if what everyone says is true, it's full of *big* fish.

Suddenly, we make a left turn around a point. At the same time, Leo takes a right, leading Uncle Vern and Dill to a different area. I hope they have good luck—but I hope we have even better luck!

We enter a bay about the size of a football field. Then the motor sound fades, and we settle into the water as if Jack had hit the brakes. In our wake, waves roll across the peaceful bay.

Looking down, I can see the bottom about ten feet below us. Even though the water is stained, it's clear.

And thanks to my cool-looking polarized sunglasses, I can see a few green weeds that look like snakes coming from the bottom. Polarized lenses magically cut through the glare of the water. They help us see fish following our lures or hiding by logs.

Just thinking about the fish we'll soon be seeing sends an electric burst of excitement through me. I'm so pumped for this! I look over at Dad, and I can see the same electricity coursing through him.

"This is a good spot," Jack says flatly. "We always get a few nice ones out of here."

He's so matter-of-fact. Dad and I are almost coming out of our skin with excitement, while Jack shows no emotion at all. I get the feeling he would be calm even if a tornado were coming down the lake right at us.

Dad and I snap into action like bees from a smacked beehive. We grab our fishing rods. Dad pops open his big green tackle box. It's filled with our favorite lures, mostly all the big ones. We're sharing one box on this trip, to save space.

"What do you want to try first, Luke?" Dad asks, eying up the lures.

"My giant red-eye spoon, for sure! The bigger the lure, the bigger the fish. That's what Grandpa always says," I add with a confident smile.

Dad hands me the golden spoon lure. I clip it onto my footlong steel leader.

A leader is a special type of thin twisted steel that you connect at the end of your regular line. These are the strongest leaders we've ever used, because the northerns up here have long razor-sharp teeth. The last thing I want is my line to break. I don't want to lose a monster fish—or my lucky spoon.

Seeing me get set with my lure, Dad then looks back at Jack. "What do you recommend I try?"

I'm surprised. Why is Dad asking for advice? He's one of the best fishermen I know.

"The water is still cold," Jack says. "I'd use something a little smaller."

Dad scans the box. There are spoons, bucktail spinners, and plugs that look just like real fish. After a few seconds, he reaches in and pulls out a red-and-white Dardevle about four inches long.

I didn't even know we brought lures that small. It's way smaller than my red-eye.

Dad holds up the Dardevle for Jack. "How's this?"

"That should work," Jack says plainly.

Once again, I get the feeling it takes a lot to get him excited.

Well, Dad can catch tiny fish with that tiny lure if he wants to. Me, I'm dying to cast out my monster red-eye and pull in monster fish.

I push the button on my sweet stainless reel. I then pull back and launch my red-eye through the air. This could be the cast that lands me the fish of a lifetime!

The red-eye hits the water with a big smack. It sounds like someone slapped the rump of a horse. I love that sound—it usually attracts fish. I picture giant northerns swimming around like a pack of hungry alligators. The second they hear prey in the water, they turn and attack!

I let the spoon sink for a second, then I start cranking fast. My heart pounds with excitement. My knuckles are white as I hold the rod tight and wait for something to strike.

As I pull my lure closer to the boat, I see the sun shining off its gold surface. It looks like little streaks of lightning. I lock my eyes on it.

When the lure is about ten feet away, I narrow my eyes and focus through my sunglasses. Suddenly, I think I see something. When my brain finally catches up with my eyes, I gasp.

There is a monster northern pike—the size of a tree trunk.

And it's following my red-eye!

Chapter 4

"Look!" I call out with both excitement and panic. "There's a monster following my lure! That thing is giant!"

Both Jack and Dad look out and see the fish. It's now right up to the boat.

"That's *huuuuge*!" Dad says, dragging out the word *huge*.

I don't know what to do. I finally decide to stop reeling and give the red-eye a jig.

Instantly, the pike turns and swims away.

"No! No! No!" I exclaim. "Why didn't he take it?" I look up to the sky, questioning and wondering.

"Oh man—that was a big one, Luke," Dad says.

"It's better if you keep your lure moving at all times," Jack says. "Do you know how to do a figure eight?"

I crunch up my mouth, crinkle my eyes, and shake my head in confusion.

"Could I borrow your rod for a second?" Jack asks Dad.

"Sure!" he replies.

Jack takes the rod and lets out about three feet of line. Then he tilts the rod down so the tip is in the water.

"Now watch as I 'draw' the number eight," he says. "Do you see it?"

My eyes follow the tip. Sure enough, I can make out the swirls and curves of an 8 shape. It's crazy. I've been fishing my whole life, yet I've never seen something like this.

"Big fish like to follow your lure right to the boat," Jack says. "They think it's a snack. And when you keep moving the lure in different directions like this, the fish think the snack is trying to escape. That's when they'll attack. And when that happens, you'd better be holding on tight."

"Thanks, Jack!" Dad says. "That's a great tip." He then turns to me and nods. "I guess you and I both just learned something, Luke."

Jack hands Dad's rod back. Without hesitating, Dad launches a cast.

I quickly cast my lure back out too—in the direction that big monster went when it swam away. I want another shot at that giant!

Dad and I reel fast, hoping to get a bite. No luck. Like machines, we reel up and send our lures through the air again.

Seconds after Dad's Dardevle hits the water, he jerks back and sets the hook.

"Got one!" he says through clenched teeth.

"Nice! Is it big?" I ask.

"It feels like a good one," he says.

After a short fight, Dad pulls in a nice five-to-six-pound northern. A nice fish—though nowhere as huge as the one we saw following my red-eye.

Jack swoops the northern into the green net. In a flash, he removes the hook and has the fish back in the water.

I give Dad a quick high five. At the same time, I can see a monster northern swimming away from our boat.

"There goes a giant one!" I say, pointing.

"Catch him!" Dad replies.

"Cast way out in front of him," Jack directs.

I pick a spot and let my red-eye fly. This could be the cast that makes it happen!

My red-eye crashes through the water. I give a count of two before cranking. With wide eyes, I reel, watch, and wait. At any second, my rod tip could go crazy with a giant northern on the other end.

Moments later, I see light flickering through the water—but no fish. A little disappointment flows through my body. I want to catch a fish so bad that it hurts.

Then, just like a heat-seeking torpedo, the monster northern darts in and races right toward my red-eye.

"He's on it!" I burst out.

"Figure eight!" Jack calls out.

I reach out and try my best to draw an eight with my rod tip. It ends up being more like a half circle.

The monster takes a swipe at my red-eye . . . but never touches it. My heart sinks as the giant races out of sight.

Why is this not working?

Chapter 5

"Come on!" I grumble, pulling my line in. "How come he didn't take it?"

"I think that spoon is a little too big," Jack says.

"Too big?" I echo. "But that fish was huge!"

Jack shakes his head. "It's not about the size of the fish. It's about the temperature of the water."

I give him a funny look.

"It's like I told your dad earlier—the water is cold. That makes the fish a little sluggish. They don't have the energy to go after big 'snacks' like that red-eye."

"But this is one of my favorite lures!" I shoot back. "I've caught a bunch of northerns on it."

"It's up to you," Jack says quietly.

He then starts the motor and slowly glides the boat across the bay.

"Keep casting," he says. "I'll move us around."

I launch a cast off the right side, and Dad sends one off the left. Both casts land about ten feet from the shorelines.

I instantly get a bite. But when I set the hook, nothing is there. Then I get another hit. I jerk back for the second time. Nothing.

"Man!" I say with a grunt. "Two hits and two misses."

Dad doesn't have time to console me. He's too busy pulling in yet another fish. This one is a five pounder.

"That was fun!" he hoots as Jack plops the fish back into the lake.

Shaking my head in frustration, I launch another cast. I'm happy for Dad, but I hate getting outfished by anyone.

As I reel, my red-eye gets pounded again. I instantly set the hook yet feel nothing. What is going on?

I keep reeling. When my sparkling spoon is in sight, I see another monster northern trailing right behind. My heart speeds up, and I go into figure-eight mode. This time, I actually make an eight.

But the fish just sits there, suspended in the water, looking at the spoon. Then it slowly swims away.

"Are you kidding me?" I say, looking at Dad and Jack.

Jack turns to Dad and tilts his head. "Is this when I remind him that the water is cold and they aren't ready to eat big things?"

In response, Dad raises his shoulders to his ears and tilts his head back at Jack. "Advice is only good if someone is willing to accept it, right?"

I'm quiet as the words sink in. Jack isn't saying that my favorite red-eye is a bad lure. He's just trying to help me understand that it's not the right lure right now.

"How long have you been guiding, Jack?" Dad asks.

"Fourteen years on this lake, plus five more years on other lakes," Jack answers.

Dad then looks over at me. "And how long have *we* been fishing on this lake, Luke?"

I let out a big sigh. "About an hour," I say. Nodding slowly, I'm starting to get the point.

Dad smiles. "Jack's job is to help us catch fish. That's what guides do. They're filled with knowledge and wisdom, and we can learn so much from them."

He leans in a little and places a hand on my shoulder.

"Haven't I always encouraged you to learn from others?" he asks me. "To seek first to understand, then seek to be understood? It's a great lesson, no matter where you are or what you are doing."

I smile back and nod some more. "Got it, Dad. Thanks for reminding me."

I take a breath, clear my throat, then speak up.

"So, Jack," I say, "what lure would you recommend I use with the current conditions?"

Dad gives me a wink.

If I'm not mistaken, the slightest hint of a smile appears on Jack's face. A second later, though, he's back to his usual blank expression.

"Do you have a Mepps Number Five?" he asks.

I pop open the tackle box and start hunting. When I get to the bottom row, my eyes light up. I see five giant Mepps spinners and one small one.

I grab the small one. It has brown hair or fur coming off the back. And sure enough, it has a number 5 on the spinner blade.

"Mepps Number Five it is!" I announce, holding the lure up like a trophy.

I quickly set myself up with the Mepps. It looks really small compared to my red-eye. But now I understand that that's a good thing.

With new hope and even more excitement, I look at Dad. "Oh baby, here we go!"

I launch the Mepps into the air. I know this cast will be the one.

With a tiny splash, the Mepps drops into the water. I give it two seconds and then start to reel. Not too fast.

All my senses are ready. My fingers are like lightning rods, ready to feel the slightest tug.

Instantly, my rod tip goes crazy. I snap back, setting the hook.

Chapter 6

"BAM!" I yell out.

The loud noise startles Jack. He flinches his shoulders like he expected to get hit by something.

"Sorry, Jack," Dad says with a little laugh. "Luke gets pretty excited when he catches a fish. I should have warned you about that!"

"This isn't a fish—it's a *monster*!" I say through clenched teeth.

"Bring him in, buddy!" Dad says, feeding off my excitement.

The fight is unbelievable. The fish takes line off my reel at will. All I can do is hold on for my life.

But then the fish slows down, allowing me to start reeling in the line. I pull back the rod, then crank. Over and over. Easing the fish forward. Never giving him any slack.

It's not like this is my first rodeo. I've done this many times with fish, but never with one this big.

Just when I think I'm making some progress, the fish makes another run for it. I grunt, pull, and hold on. This is epic!

"You're doing great," Dad coaches. "Keep workin' him."

Out of the corner of my eye, I see Dad turn to Jack for confirmation. Jack gives a thumbs-up and a single nod. That makes me feel good. I must be doing everything right.

At last, the monster is close enough for us to see him. He's *huge*! It looks like I'm pulling in a tree trunk.

"That's a good one," Jack says calmly.

What an understatement.

I continue to fight. My arms are starting to wear out, but there's no way I will let this fish beat me. I bear down and draw in a big breath to build my strength.

This last burst of willpower is working. I can feel it on the other end of the line—the fish is getting tired.

Once I get the fish really close, Jack reaches for the net. "See if you can work him over to me," he says.

I pull up and toward Jack. Once again, it's like I'm dragging a dead log through the water.

With one quick scoop, Jack has the exhausted monster in the net.

"Yes!" Dad and I yell at the same time.

Jack uses his pliers to snap the hook out of the giant mouth full of sharp teeth. He quickly lays the fish on the bottom of the boat and measures it with his white tape.

"Thirty-four inches," he announces.

"Wow!" Dad exclaims. "That's a nice one!"

Jack picks up the fish and hands it over to me. I carefully take it in my two hands and cradle it into my life jacket.

This monster is heavy! But thank goodness he's tired. He lies still in my arms. The last thing we need is for this giant to go crazy and start thrashing around.

Dad has his phone ready to snap a picture. He doesn't have to tell me to smile. I'm already grinning from ear to ear.

Once we've got a couple of shots, Jack guides me as we get the monster back into the water. I've done this before with other

big fish, so I know how careful we need to be.

After a few seconds, the fish gives his tail a powerful swipe, smacking the side of the boat, then propels through my hands.

"Be free, big guy!" I call out.

I watch as it fades away from my sight, but not my memory.

After rinsing the slime off my hands in the cold water, I look over at Dad with a proud smile. He holds up his right hand, and I give him a crushing high five.

"That was awesome!" I sit down with a thud.

"Yes, it was!" Dad confirms.

"And thanks, Jack," I add. "Great call on the lure." I give him a smile too.

He gives me a thumbs-up. No smile.

I accept that.

"Well," Dad says, "let's get after 'em. That sure was a monster, but maybe there are even *bigger* ones out there. Maybe we'll even get luckier!" He winks.

An excited chill runs down my spine. I suddenly remember that strange feeling I got when we flew in over the lake. I knew it then— this wild, beautiful lake is full of surprises and mysteries. Like Dad said, maybe we'll be lucky enough to catch something even more amazing than that beast I hauled in.

'Cause if there is one thing I've been called, it's Lucky!

49

My fingers tingle with anticipation as I ready my rod. I'm just about to cast—but then I hear something. The hum of a motor.

I look over to see Leo, Uncle Vern, and Dill cruising our way. I can't wait to hear about what they've caught.

Chapter 7

Leo brings their boat to a stop near ours. They glide through the water like an iceberg at the North Pole.

"How's it going, guys?" I call over. My voice echoes off the water and the surrounding pine trees.

"Great!" Dill shoots back.

As the two boats drift aimlessly but closer together, we start swapping stories back and forth. Dill tells me all about the decent-sized northerns they've been landing, and I fill him in on our adventures.

As we compare notes, we learn that my thirty-four-incher is by far the biggest anyone has caught today. Of course, that makes sense, given what Jack said about the water being too cold for big northerns. From the sound of it, my big one was a lucky catch. I can't hide my pride.

Once our chatter dies down, Dad looks to Jack and then Leo. "So, what do you guys have in store for us next?"

"Should we head down to the secret spot?" Jack asks Leo.

A big smile grows on Leo's face. "Do you think they're ready?"

"They know how to fish. They're ready," Jack replies in his usual calm manner.

"Then let's do it!" Leo says with some gusto.

As both motors rev back to life, Dill and I look at each other with wild smiles flaring. We cannot wait to get to this secret spot!

Jack takes the lead as we race out to the main water and hook a left. Leo, Uncle Vern, and Dill follow right behind us.

After a fifteen-minute cruise down the lake, we ease into a big bay. There isn't a breath of wind here. The water is like glass. I can see the bottom, about ten feet down. There are a bunch of giant boulders and big rocks down there, but not many weeds.

"All right, let's get those lines in the water!" Dad announces to the whole group. "The hunt for the biggest fish is on!"

"Good luck, Dill and Uncle Vern!" I say.

"You too!" Dill chimes back.

"So, thirty-four inches is the number to beat—right, Luke?" Uncle Vern calls over.

"Yeah, but I plan on catching an even bigger one!" I say with a proud smile.

I'm not sure that's possible in this cold water. But you never know what can happen.

I want to beat everyone to the punch and be the first line in the water. Lightning-quick, I launch a cast. My Mepps Number Five lands with a tiny splash and breaks the glass.

After just a few cranks—BAM!—my lure gets nailed. With a grunt and a quick smile, I set the hook.

"Fish on!" I say loud enough for Dill and Uncle Vern to hear.

"Yeehaw!" Dill hoots.

This northern has lots of spunk. I fight it and eventually pull it closer to the boat. It's a nice six-pounder.

"That's a good way to start," Dad says.

Suddenly, out of nowhere, a truly monstrous fish comes darting in. It's even bigger and way fatter than my thirty-four-incher. This new beast with supersized jaws grabs hold of my northern.

"Whoa!" I gasp as my rod is almost ripped out of my hands.

In a second, the monster lets go and darts off.

I'm frozen in shock. It takes me a few seconds to even form words. "What in the world was *that*!" I exclaim.

Dad's eyes are as wide and wild as mine. We're both stunned as we look at the streaks of blood in the water.

Jack, though, is as unruffled as ever. "That," he says, "was a monster lake trout."

Chapter 8

"*Monster lake trout?*" I repeat.

Jack nods. "They usually live in one hundred feet of water. But each spring, when the water is just the right temperature, they move into the shallows and feed on the northerns. That's what this one was doing—he was trying to steal your fish."

"Wait a minute," I say, scratching my head. "Did you say the water temperature is 'just right' now?"

Jack bobs his head. "Yep. It's too cold for big northerns, but it's just right for big lake trout. So, this might just be your lucky day. Lake trout are fun to go after. They fight harder than any fish."

Jack sends one perfect whistle toward the other boat to get Leo's attention. "Lake trout," Jack says loudly.

Leo gives Jack a nod. With a growing smile on his face, he then turns to Uncle Vern and Dill. In seconds, I see them scrambling for new lures.

We fly into action too. Dad immediately opens up our tackle box and shows it to Jack.

"What do you recommend?" Dad asks.

After a short glance, Jack points at two spoons—an all-silver Dardevle and a yellow-and-red Five of Diamonds.

"I'll try the yellow one!" I say.

In seconds, we gear up. We're ready to take on the lake trout. My heart is beating right out of my chest. I'm more excited than I ever thought possible.

What a turn of events! We came here for monster northerns, but now we've discovered other monsters to go after. Just as I'd predicted—there are all sorts of mysteries in this water. You never know what each adventure will bring you. All you can do is just be ready to roll with it.

"Let's do this!" I say.

I give Dad a knuckle punch. Maybe a little too hard.

With that, I launch a long cast and start cranking. Dad does the same.

We don't get any bites on our first few casts. I'm still pumped, but a little bit of doubt seeps in every time we reel in an empty line. Where are these monsters?

Then, Dad jerks back like he's been stung by a bee. He sets the hook.

Just like that, we are in the game!

Dad starts to pull in the fish, but the fish has other plans. Dad's rod bends down to the water, his drag screams, and his line races into the water. It's like he has hooked onto a moving truck, not a fish.

"Wow!" Dad says. His smile makes it clear he's having a blast, but his eyes are still filled with a mix of confusion and excitement. "Is this one of those lake trout?" he asks in a grunting voice as he holds on with all he has.

"Probably," Jack says simply.

"Pull him in! You got this!" Dill screams from the other boat. They are close enough to see all the action.

I reel in and set my rod down so I can focus on Dad. I don't care how long it takes. The minutes fly by in a blur as Dad and the trout fight their mighty battle. Dad said he wants to catch the fish of a lifetime, and this might just be it.

Slowly but surely, Dad tires out the monster. It takes twenty minutes, but he pulls the behemoth closer and closer to the boat.

At last, we see a flash of orange and black in the water. Dad and I both gasp.

"Oh, baby. This is serious," Dad says. He lets out a haunting laugh.

I shake my head. I think he's losing his mind! I haven't seen him this excited since I shot my first turkey.

"What's happening over there?" Dill calls out. "Do you see it yet?"

I lean over and hold on to the edge of the boat to get a better view.

"It's *huge*!" I exclaim. "Just like a big fat tree trunk." I hold out my hands, way apart, to signal the size of this monster.

Dad pulls the exhausted fish over to Jack, who's ready with the net.

"Come on, come on," I nervously urge. "Get him into the net!"

Jack, of course, is cool as a cucumber. In a second, he scoops up the monster trout.

"YES!" I shout, raising my hands high.

I'm still holding up my arms as I look over at Dill and Uncle Vern. Their arms go up in victory to join me.

Jack pops out the hook and quickly measures and weighs the fish. "Twenty-three pounds," he announces. "And thirty-eight and a half inches long."

Dad's mouth drops open. "That's the biggest fish I have ever caught!"

With his straight face, Jack nods. "Yep. It's a good one."

Once Jack carefully hands the giant over to Dad, I quickly grab the phone and snap several pictures.

Dad then leans over and begins easing the giant back into the water. He watches the fish as it slides through his fingers. I feel like Dad is trying to lock the fish into his memory.

Once the monster disappears, Dad turns to me, and we smack a high five. Water from his wet hand sprays out and covers my glasses.

"That was amazing," he says, letting out a big breath and plopping back down on his seat.

"Totally!" I reply. "And now *I* have to catch one like that!"

With superhero strength, I launch a mile-long cast. I have a feeling—this could be the one.

Halfway to the boat, my spoon gets nailed.

Chapter 9

"Gotcha!" I shout as I set the hook.

Instantly, my line flows out like water from a hose. Then my drag starts to scream. Whatever is on the other end of this line is *big* and full of fight. I've never felt anything like it.

"Oh boy!" I say through clenched teeth. "That's what I'm talkin' about!"

"Yep—that's a good one," Jack says. "That's the one you've been looking for."

Finally, my line stops. At last, I can start cranking line back in. Inch by inch, I pull the fish in.

"Come on, Lucky Luke!" Dad says. "You can do it! Pull that monster in!"

I look over at him with wild, excited eyes. I'm smiling from ear to ear.

Just then, the fish makes another run for it. All I can do is hold on.

"*Ohhh*, baby!" I sing.

I let the line run until it stops, then I crank and pull. My left arm burns, but there's no way I'm gonna give up or give in to this fish. I bear down and keep cranking and fighting.

I'm in total go-mode. I've caught hundreds of fish, and they've all prepared me for this moment. This is the battle of my life.

"Get him, Luke!" Dill yells over.

I look over to see him, Uncle Vern, and even Leo standing in their boat, watching the whole show.

Crank and fight. Crank and fight. On and on it goes until—finally—I get a glimpse of that magical orange-and-black body.

"There he is!" I say, still clenching my teeth.

"*She*," Jack calmly corrects. "That's a big one, so it's a female."

"You're doing great, Luke," Dad chimes in. "Get her in. She's tired now."

Out of the corner of my eye, I see Jack slide the net out.

"Bring her to me when you can," he says. "Nice and steady."

Jack's right—I need to take my time with these final steps. After battling with this monster for what seems like forever, the last thing I want to do is lose her inches from the boat. So, I ease up just a bit. Not too fast. Not too slow. I hold my breath as I pull her toward Jack and the waiting net.

But the trout isn't buying it. Suddenly, she races away, taking my line with her for the third time.

I groan, and so does Dad. Even Jack lets out a noise, which isn't normal.

"I guess she isn't done yet, huh?" Jack says.

"Nope!" I say, letting out a big breath.

After an Olympic-like sprint, the line stops. Now it's time to do it all over again. I have to crank the monster back in.

Only, my left hand and arm are toast. I take a second to shake it out, hoping to bring some life back into it. Once I feel some tingling, I start cranking.

"Here we go again . . ." I say.

I hope this behemoth doesn't have any more runs in her. I'm getting tired. But that means she must be getting tired too.

Sure enough, she doesn't put up nearly as much fight this time. It's still a battle, though—a battle to see which one of us will outlast the other.

"Luke, this is one of those moments when you get to decide how much you have in your tank," Dad says. "So, dig deep. See what you're made of!" He gives me an encouraging smile.

With that, new energy surges inside me. After a few big cranks, I see the orange-and-black flash. She's on her way. I'm going to win this battle!

Jack readies the net. "Easy . . . Easy . . ." His voice quivers a little. "You don't want your line to break. You're so close!"

I look over at him, and his smile is almost as big as mine. I can't believe it. Now even *Jack* is excited. This is awesome!

I don't even dare to breathe as I ease the fish up and over to the big green net. Jack scoops the monster and lifts her out of the water.

And just like that, it's done.

Dad, Dill, Uncle Vern, and Leo all cheer and pump their arms in the air. Jack just grins.

Overwhelmed with both exhaustion and excitement, I collapse into my seat and let my rod drop out of my hand. It's all I can do to raise my arms up in victory.

"*Whoo-weee!*" I shout.

From that point on, everything feels like a blur. Jack measures and weighs my trout. She is thirty-nine inches and twenty-four pounds. I can barely lift her up for the other guys to see.

We take some quick pictures, and then, in a blink, the giant is back in the water. I let all thirty-nine inches of her slip through my fingers.

The whole time, I feel like I'm floating in a dream. I can't stop grinning. This has clearly turned into one of the greatest adventures of my life.

"Luke, that was a huge fish!" Dill yells over.

"That wasn't a huge fish," I reply. "That was a MONSTER!"

About the Author

Kevin Lovegreen was born and raised in Minnesota. His loving wife, Sue and two amazing children, Crystal and Luke all share their love for the outdoors. Hunting and fishing have always been a big part of Kevin's life. From chasing squirrels as a child to chasing elk as an adult, Kevin loves the thrill of the adventure. But even more, he loves telling the stories. Presenting at schools and connecting with kids is one of his favorite things to do.

Monster Mule Deer

Lucky Luke's
25 lb. turkey

The
Muddy
Elk

Crystal'
1st buc

Lucky Luke
with a large-
mouth bass

Lucky Luke's
1st bear

Crystal, The Swamp hero!

www.KevinLovegreen.com

Other books in the series

AR-rated
(Accelerated Reader)

Award-winning

LUCKY LUKE'S ADVENTURES

Dear reader,

I hope you enjoyed the adventure!

All the stories in the Lucky Luke's Adventure series are based on real experiences. And I truly believe they all happened so I could write you these books.

If you like this book, please help spread the word by telling all your friends.

Keep being amazing!

Kevin Lovegreen

**The More You Read,
The Smarter You Get!**